Poetry in God's Words
Alpha-Omega

Doris Shackelford-Dozier

authorHOUSE®

AuthorHouse™
1663 Liberty Drive
Bloomington, IN 47403
www.authorhouse.com
Phone: 1 (800) 839-8640

Published by AuthorHouse   04/27/2015

ISBN: 978-1-5049-0407-0 (sc)
ISBN: 978-1-5049-0406-3 (e)

Print information available on the last page.

Any people depicted in stock imagery provided by Thinkstock are models, and such images are being used for illustrative purposes only. Certain stock imagery © Thinkstock.

Scripture quotations marked KJV are from the Holy Bible, King James Version (Authorized Version). First published in 1611. Quoted from the KJV Classic Reference Bible, Copyright © 1983 by The Zondervan Corporation.

This book is printed on acid-free paper.

Contents

INTRODUCTION 1
GOD'S PROMISE 2
MY SHIELD... 4
THE FALL OF MAN 6
LORD, YOU CREATED ME... 8
YOUR LIFE.. 10
DEATH.. 12
HATE.. 14
BEEN THERE 16
BUT, GOD YOU SAID 18
CHRISTIAN... 20
WHAT GOES AROUND, COMES AROUND....................... 22
SUCCESS 24
MY FAMILY TREE.. 26
RE-RAISING A GROWN CHILD 28
REASON FOR THE SEASON 30
SUNDAY 32
IMITATION OF LIFE 34
LIAR 36
STAND FOR SOMETHING OR FALL FOR ANYTHING 38
A BRUSH WITH DEATH... 40
WHICH WAY 42
A SINNER'S CRY.. 44
BLIND MAN.. 46
ATTITUDE... 48
CHOSEN ONE 50
DEPRESSED 52
SUICIDE... 54
THIN LINE 56
BELIEVER 58
PURPOSE IN LIFE... 60
THE HAND THAT LIFE DEALT YOU 62
MAKING A STATEMENT 64
HOW WELL DO CHILDREN LISTEN................................ 66
MOTHER OF A TRICKSTER.. 68
WELL DONE 70
HE GIVES YOU BUSINESS OF YOUR OWN 72
CONDITION OF A MAN... 74
SEASONAL FRIEND... 76
THE REVEREND DR. MARTIN LUTHER KING.................. 78

SLEEP 80
LIFE 82
HAPPINESS 84
CREATION 86
CHURCH PEOPLE 88
ENEMY 90
DEVIL 92
ORDER OUR STEPS 94
THIS HOUSE 96
TOMORROW 98
WHO ARE YOU 100
BORN 102
OUR FATHER 104
HOW DARE DO YOU BE DIFFERENT 106
IF I 110
BELIEVES 112
STARTING OVER 114
DRUGS 116
AGE IS ONLY A NUMBER 118
DRIVING 120
MAN WITH A PLAN 122
AMERICA 124
OUR STEPS ARE ORDERED 126
WHEN I CRY 128
GOOD-BYE 130
FROWN 132
INTELLIGENCE verses IGNORANCE 134
RELATIONSHIP 136
CHANGE 138
DECISIONS 140
A WISE MAN 142
GOOD NIGHT 144
LAUGH OR CRY 146
MEMORIES 148
IN TIMES OF SORROW 150
GOOD OLE DAYS 152
ON THE OUTSIDE LOOKING IN 154
TRUE FRIENDSHIP 156
PARANOID 158
A DEVIL AT EVERY LEVEL 160
HEAR MY CRY 162
HALF GROWN ROSE 164
STAND 166
BLINDSIDE 168
GOOD TEACHERS 170

LATERAL ENTRY TEACHER 172
SISTERS 174
HOMELESS 176
STARTING OVER 178
OLD AGE 180
MIRROR IMAGES 182
WHEN A STRANGER CALLS 184
LEADERSHIP 186
MENTAL CLOSET 188
ENDURANCE 190
FAMILY 192
MAKING DECISIONS 194
DREAMS 196
YES 198
GOD 200
GOD REIGNS 202
THE OLD TESTAMENT 204
THE NEW TESTAMENT 205
GLOSSARY 207

INTRODUCTION

Nature verses nurture has been a force that I have struggle with since birth. But, in July 2014 I came full term with the true definition of these two words that had my soul, mind, and spirit in bondage for 60 years. Losing my mother at an early age (2) and rare by an Aunt in South Carolina; I got lost/caught up and confused in my own world. I wore a great beautiful smile on the outside whereas people viewed me as happy. Lord, on the inside where the world could not see; stood that large deep empty hole in my heart, mind, and inner spirit. Many days I spent in God's present crying, tears full of despair, mental pain, hurt, and loneliness....

Through it all, GOD lifted me. He allowed me to marry, have three healthy children, and held a career. The roads were rough for me. The mental impact came full force when I was forty-three years old. I did not know what was happening to me because my mental anguish came out in physical pain. The medical doctors were looking for a physical diagnose and all along it was mental. Those lost years left me between a mental rock and a hard dark place. Strong, I would always overcome the mental moment and moved to the next chapter in my life until my mental life came full circle.

I hid my mental aguish by working hard and being the best employee any agency can have. Little that I know; I worked hard not to get the job done, but to keep the Boss in my favor. Well that worked fine until March 1995: I was physically sick and while taking time off to heal; my supervisor and my co-workers decided to sabotage my work ethics. Under doctor's care, I was forced to go to work sick. For two weeks I was forced to work under hostile condition; I literally refused to speak to them during that period. On March 22, 1995, I lost it; my whole world crumbled. From that point, I had to take ownership with my true purpose in life. I refused to talk about it, so I started writing. Putting my true feelings on paper was the result of me dealing with life, meaning that: "It is what it is' deal with it' or it will deal with you". Yes, MY SPIRITUAL SELF REALIZATION.

The tangible dualities (such as, light or dark, high or low, hot or cold, fire or water, go or stop, life or death and so on...) Knowing the differences of these tangible dualities made me aware of my life purpose. My contribution to life is this book, how it has helped me and I pray that it can be of great help to others as well. I give GOD all the GLORY...I am just a vessel that God has chosen this book to flow through.

GOD'S PROMISE

GOD'S great ordinance is a divine decree
A law made for both you and me
Written in red for everyone to see
He created the heaven and the earth
Orders our steps prior to birth
He knows us for exactly who we are
Capable of seeing just that far
Put Him first in everything that you do
It's a Promise that GOD will take care of you

GOD'S promise will not be broken
Cannot be replace by money nor token
We must observe all things that He commands
Being obedient will keep us in His hands
By His grace, we were placed on this land
Through the labor of a woman and aid of a man
Little that we know, we were all in His plan
He is Alpha and Omega, the beginning and the end
God Almighty! He truly will occupy this earth again

God: Alpha (**A** or **a)**) and Omega (Ω or ω)**),** (The Beginning and the End).

Genesis 1:1 "In the ___*beginning*___ God created the heavens and the earth."

MY SHIELD

The Lord is my shepherd I shall not want
The 23 Psalm teaches me all about His do's and don'ts
Daily, I walk through the valley of the shadow of death
He is always with me; therefore, I fear no evil or threat

His rod and staff they comfort me
Protects me from things that I cannot see
As I sit in the presence of my enemies
He protects me to the utmost extremities

His goodness and mercy guides my life
Keeps me away from backbiting and strife
I will serve the Lord forever
To help me face life's endeavors

Shield: Conceal or shelter somebody or something from view.

Psalms 3:3 "But thou, O LORD, art a _**shield**_ for me; my glory, and the lifter up of mine head."

THE FALL OF MAN

God formed man in his own image from the dust of the ground
Took his rib and made a woman perfectly sound
He called them Adam and Eve and let them roam unbounded
The history of His wonderful creation spread all around

How God made man and woman is very hard to believe
He was pleased, but only moments away from being deceived
Adam and Eve sins caused them to wear fig leaves
Eventually, they got together and twin boys were conceived

They named one Cain and the other Abel
Unlike baby Jesus, they were not born in a stable
Because of Adam and Eve's sin, their sons had to labor
Introduction to death when Cain slew his brother Abel

Man's time is short upon this land
Cain killed Abel by a blow of his hand
His life was shortened just before he became a man
Abel's body perished into the ground and became sand

God forgives us seventy and sevenfold
Eve bit the fruit and when asked; she never told
He granted her another son, this she had to unfold
All our sins are revealed whether our bodies are hot or cold

The truth, shall always be told by man
As long as he occupies God's land
We need to take a spiritual stand
So that we would not fall by man's hand

Nation: A large group of people who share a common language, culture, ethnicity, descent, or history.

Genesis 25:23   "And the LORD said unto her, Two ***nations*** *are* in thy womb, and two manner of people shall be separated from thy bowels; and the one people shall be stronger than the *other* people; and the elder shall serve the younger."

LORD, YOU CREATED ME

Lord, you created me into the person that you wanted me to be
Although my mother and father conceived me
But, You drew the final picture for everyone to see
People still complain, knowing that they cannot do better than Thee

We are never satisfied with your great work
Constantly sit around, complaining and acting like Jerks
Everything that we say or do; leaves a question mark geared towards you
Where we should be grateful that you did not make us in the form of two

Some said you made them too tall, some said too small
I know you wonder why you bother to make them at all
If we would just be still, listen, and answer your call
We all would be better off overall

You made some of us blind and some that can see
But when it comes to doing your work, where are we?
What we do not know is that your work is meant to be
Whether we know or not, you created us can't we see?

Lord, you gave some of us voices to speak
But, when it comes to spreading your word, we have a leak
We do not have to scream to our highest peak
Because your work can be shown without the use of our beaks

I know that you created me
I do not have to be tall or small or speak or see
But I would live your word and be a good example for Thee
And everyone would know what you created me to be

Christit: The anointed ONE.

Galatians 2:20   "I am crucified with ***Christ***: nevertheless I live; yet not I, but Christ liveth in me: and the life which I now live in the flesh I live by the faith of the Son of God, who loved me, and gave himself for me."

YOUR LIFE

Life is short, innocent, and sweet
Some live it lying down and some on their feet
It is a gamble with a bet, not controlled by saying can I; or let
These negative words turn life into a threat

In life you can be anything that you choose to be
As long as you don't put your trust in man or me
Others will steal your joy don't you see
But, true comfort of life lies within thee

Live life to the fullest each day
Do not allow anyone to be the reason for your delay
When it comes to your life no one should have a say
Their opinions would hinder you in every way

Even the smallest intervention is like running a relay
Always stay focus and remain at bay
Tomorrow is not promise, it is as shaded as the color gray
When it all boils down, only you can live your life, so start today

Life: Characteristic that distinguishes organisms from inorganic substances.

Leviticus 17:11 "For the *life* of the flesh is in the blood: and I have given it to you upon the alter to make an atonement for your souls:"

DEATH

Death is destined; it comes to everyone
No one knows the day or the hour
Each moment should be cherish like there is no tomorrow
Time cannot be bought or borrow
Fills the heart with pain and very hollow
It always leave the love ones with despair and sorrow

If you think that life is done when death comes upon
Listen! Maybe, you have just created room for someone
We cannot explain when death takes place
For all we know it can create a new race
Death is not controlled by anyone's pace
But, in some of us, it is clearly painted on our face

Some people eat, exercise and try to do the right thing
But, death still will come, and with a sting
We pray, cry, laugh, and wallow
But, it will still consumes us with a swift swallow
Now, we can't run and we can't hide
Death is a part of life and it is always by our side

Death: Cessation of all biological functions that sustain a living organism.

Psalm 23:4   "Yea, though I walk through the valley of the shadow of **_death_**, I will fear no evil: for thou *art* with me; thy rod and thy staff they comfort me."

HATE

Hate is a game that you should negate
Its action will take you straight to Hell's gate
The result can cause your heart and soul to separate
So, please cleanse your mind before it is too late

Hate causes a son to hurt his father
A daughter to fight her mother
Brings life-long silence between sisters and brothers
It even makes people kill one another

Hate causes you pain and sorrow
It stops your dreams and silence your tomorrow
A sickness you cannot steal or borrow
Replace it with love, so others will follow

Hate puts you in a world that is so unreal
You have to go through a long process to heal
After the process, you can say; life has dealt you a new deal
Suddenly, the world and people around you seems so real

Hate: To feel intense, dislike or extreme aversion of hostility.

Matthew 6:24   "No man can serve two masters: for either he will ***hate*** the one, and love the other; or else he will hold to the one, and despise the other. Ye cannot serve God and mammon."

BEEN THERE

I have been there and done that too
Here try it on; it's my personal shoes
I have been to the mountain, above hell's top
Life's circumstances kept me there until God said stop

In a lifetime there are so many roads to travel
On my way there, I fought various devils
I knew in order to get there, I had to keep my head level
The tight knots that kept me bound, I had to unravel

They did this and they did that to me
Things they thought that I could not see
I kept my eyes focused high on the Almighty
He smoothed those rough roads that meant to be

When bad things happened, I knew it was the work of two or three
In fighting those battles, it only took God and me
I was set up so perfectly, it was too hard to deny, so I took the rap you see
But through the whole struggle, I knew that salvation was free

One day there were things that I wanted them to hear
But, God said, hush child; there are still more that you have to bare
So, I sat there for two weeks and did nothing but stare
As I waited patiently, God said to me, this is not rare

The wound became so deep; I was awake, yet asleep
For several days all I could do was take a peek
I refused to speak but was sharp to hear
I heard the Master said: I am still with you my dear

I knew if I had said one spoken word and had been heard
My career would have pass me by, higher than the birds
The tension got so high; I thought that I was going to die
I realized that the whole time that I was living a lie

To maintain my sanity; for days I resided to my bed
Refused to eat; not even self or forcefully fed
Without any notice, God snatched me up, not a word was said
At that moment I knew that I was Holy Spirit led

Endure: Undergo hardship especially without giving in.

Psalm 30:5   "For his anger *endureth* but a moment; in his favour is life: weeping may **_endure_** for a night, but joy *cometh* in the morning."

BUT, GOD YOU SAID

At an early age, I questioned God, why did you do this to me
He said child: I do things and pray that you are able to see
Believe me; all my plans are destined to be
No respect to a person, I am God Almighty

I created the heaven, the seas, and land
I sputtered in the dust of the ground and formed man
Don't you know that everyone will return to sand
So, don't question me on who I am

Yes, your mother is dead!
I punched her number and made her bed
There is nothing else that can be said
She paid her debt to be heavenly laid

Child, I hear you crying
Very upset about your mother dying
She has earned her wings and is up in heaven flying
Dry your tears, later in life you would find out why I created the sky

On earth you will never see her again; I only made one Lassiter
I call those things as though they were; she is now with her Comforter
Do my work while you are on earth and one day you will see your mother
But, God you said… and I believe in You, the FATHER

Overcomed: Third-person singular simple present indicative form of overcome.

Revelation 2:7 "He that hath an ear, let him hear what the Spirit saith unto the churches; To him that ***overcometh*** will I give to eat of the tree of life, which is in the midst of the paradise of God."

CHRISTIAN

I accept the things that I cannot change
Since baptism, my life has not been the same
I am Christ-like and spiritually tame
I putted away all of my childish games
I do things in order, decently, and without shame
In everything that I do, I exalt His Name

I worship and pray with all my might
I humble myself all day and night
Faith cometh by hearing and not by sight
Therefore, I departed from iniquity without a fight
His grace and mercy allows me to do what's right
Since I became a Christian, I sleep peacefully at night

Christian_: Person who adheres to Christianity.

1 Peter 4:16   "Yet if *any man suffer* as a ___Christian___, let him not be ashamed; but let him glorify God on this behalf."

WHAT GOES AROUND, COMES AROUND

What goes around, comes around
Life is very concrete, but never sound
In this limited time on earth, we encounter many ups and downs
But when we fall, the drop is never lower than the ground

We gossip about this and that
Saying whatever comes to mind, despite the facts
Not monitoring, conversations such as you, he, she, or they say
Knowing this kind of talk brings anger that will never go away

If you tell me your secret, I will tell you mine
Not realizing, once someone other than you know, it is no longer refined
Operating in a two or three way circle is never fine
Because what goes around, comes around in just a matter of time

Wait: Indicates that one is eagerly impatient to do something or for something to happen.

Lamentations 3:26   "*It is* good that *a man* should both hope and quietly <u>***wait***</u> for the salvation of the LORD."

SUCCESS

You finally made it, soon to graduate
It took you a long time, but it is never too late
It cost a lot of money and a whole lot of faith
But, in May; you will march out of UNCC's gate

From K to twelfth, you went to school
During your first year of college, you acted a fool
Even picked up smoking, thinking that it was cool
But came to your senses, before you break any major rules

You seemed so happy when you came home
It was hard comparing your old room to your college dorm
Right then, your life had taken a new form
A few days after being home, you decided to roam

You had a choice, get your own place or live at home
But, life and its twist did not keep you away very long
During that time, thank God you chose the calmer storm
Responsible for your own actions, you had to reform

You stayed home for a year that was too much
Did not know what to do with your life, as such
By then you were over twenty-one and grown you see
Advice, oh no you refused to take it from me

You enrolled in a class at FSU, blind and without a clue
A long slow summer, but it gave you something to do
This push came from someone that you loved and knew
Sorry, the lessons learned; you cannot undo

After the summer semester at a college out of state
You came to your senses and made it back to UNCC's gate
From that point on your life was not a debate
In May you will be graduating and everyone feels great

Success*:*   The fact of getting or achieving wealth, respect, or fame.

Joshua 1:8   "This book of the law shall not depart out of thy mouth; but thou shalt meditate therein day and night, that thou mayest observe to do according to all that is written therein: for then thou shall make thy way prosperous, and then thou shalt have good ***success.***"

MY FAMILY TREE

To me my family tree was a mystery
I did not know anyone, so I started with me
I wrote names of people that I would never see
A part of my tree, they were soon to be

My mother, I know not
She is gone, but her love I have not forgot
The only memory that I have is her lying on a cot
My life has been empty as an upside down pot

The pain got deeper by the age of five
I was the one next to the last to arrive
Out of her seven children, only six survived
Between God and our aunt, we stayed well and alive

At age sixteen, she ended kicking all of us out of the door
Said in an angry voice, I don't want to see you all anymore
When I left, her youngest child was only four
The thought of leaving him, tears began to flow

This situation forced me to pray and stay on my knees
At 21, I turned over life's new leaves
To my surprise, several members of my family were bereaved
I began to grieve, took medication, but still was not relieved

I went to the doctor one particular day
Personal questions that he asked, I refused to stay
That moment I promised that I would have the final say
I knew that the answers were in South Carolina and I was on my way

Finding my descendents I was told that it could not be done
I was even told that it was a situation that could not be won
Putting a family tree together is not easy you see
But, the secret is to just start with number one (me)

Family: A group of people affiliated by consanguinity affinity.

Genesis 28:14 "And thy seed shall be as the dust of the earth, and thou shalt spread abroad to the west, and to the east, and to the north, and to the south: and in thee and in thy seed shall all the *__families__* of the earth be blessed."

RE-RAISING A GROWN CHILD

How easy do you think it is to re-raise a grown child?
One, thirteen, twenty-one these numbers you cannot re-dial
Twenty-one years you walked with them thousands of miles
Time has come for you to put up your parental files

As much as you did for them, very few depart with a smile
But when trouble comes, they pick the phone up and you they dial
Not recognizing their voices because they have not called in awhile
The tone of their voices sound so meek and mild

For years they didn't hear you, not even when you preached
Wisdom and understanding are so far from their reach
But, when trouble comes their worries increase
Putting life in perspective, their memories decrease

Never try to re-raise a grown child
They will become disrespectful and rather wild
At age twenty-one put away their growth file
If they come back, treat them kindly and in an adult style

Child: A human between the stages of birth and puberty.

Proverbs 22:6   "Train up a ___child___ in the way he should go: and when he is old, he will not depart from it."

REASON FOR THE SEASON

Christ suffered for our sins
Long ago before the world begin
He appeared in the form of a Spirit
Born to the Virgin Mary

They named Him Baby Jesus
His original name was not pleasing
They said, He shall be called EM-MAN-UEL
Counselor, Prince of Peace, or Wonderful

He was born on Christmas Day
In a manger padded with hay
This event, man did not have a say
They came from near and far just to see Him and pray

In their journey the sky was dark and gray
But the northern star got them there without a delay
They did not wonder nor go astray
Avoided all obstacles that got in their way

The Father, the Son, and the Holy Ghost
By any name, He is the most Highest and Utmost
His life was taken for the sake of us
A promise that one day, we all would return to dust

Season: A time or periods marked by particular weather conditions into which the year is traditionally divided.

Acts 1:7   "And he said unto them, It is not for you to know the times or the times or the _**seasons**_, which the Father hath put in his own power."

SUNDAY

My Labor is not in vain in the Lord
I work Holy everyday putting my trust only in God
Life can be rough, sharper than a sword
My life today is in order because I was not spared the rod

I worship my Savior everyday Saturday through Monday
But, I always serve Him in church on Sundays'
In our house the Sabbath was never a fun day
We often consider naming it "Bible's Way"

On Sundays we were not allowed to sew, swear, iron, or dance
But, we were allowed to have company and romance
We strolled along the countryside as we made our way to the park
Always focusing on the sunset, because we had to be home by dark

Simple problems we solved face to face
No, my labor is never in vain
Not now, tomorrow, or even back then
I will continue to work for God until the end

Sunday: In Christian tradition, the day set aside for the Sabbath.

Mark 2:27   "And he said unto them, The ***sabbath*** was made for man, and not man for the ***sabbath***."

IMITATION OF LIFE

When I think of the imitation of life
Only one thing comes to mind and that is strife
We are forced to make decisions, wrong or right
Some are made in the dark, others in the light
Either way, it causes us to fight or flight
Hustle and bustle with these demons all day and night

Some people are upset about their color
Which we were born without consent from one another
Light skinned blacks are often called yellow
Dark skinned whites are considered other
Fashion Fair and Mary Kay help make our day
Daily application of makeup has the last say

If you are white, wearing plain lotion is no fun
You have to apply tanning lotion and sit in the sun
Cold cream is not enough if you are dark
Wait; use Vantex, it is a good start
Some of us are scared with birthmarks
Everyone has a twin that can't be told apart

We all are imitations of life, don't we see
No one's perfect, not them, you, or me
Always changing ourselves to what we want to be
Being content with life can set us free
Will we ever reach that point, maybe!
The answer to that question comes from Thee

Inward: Relating to or existing in the mind or spirit.

2 Corinthians 4:16   "For which cause we faint not; but through our outward man perish, yet the ***inward*** *man* is renewed day by day."

LIAR

A liar tells lies and cannot be trusted
In a matter of time, he will be busted
Just to hear him talk makes you disgusted
Every time he speaks you want to say, "Hush it,"

A liar cannot tell the same story the same way twice
It is as rare as consistently rolling sevens with a dice
You don't know if to treat a liar, mean or nice
Because he feels that he needs no ones advice

A liar will give himself away every time
Quicker than the drop of a dime
His lies will begin to sound like rhymes
As he captures his audience with his chimes

So don't tell lies thinking that it is cute
All you have to do is to tell the truth
Because a lie will always be a lie
And a liar may end up in a lawsuit

Liar:　　　　Someone that tells lies.

Psalm 116:11　"I said in my haste, All men *are **<u>liars</u>**.*"

STAND FOR SOMETHING
OR FALL FOR ANYTHING

As a youngster, I have always heard people say
Child, you have to stand for something or fall for anything
Love, hate, happiness, sadness are the four main things that life brings
Whichever you choose, it leaves you with a sting

Love is like eternal burning fire
It brands the heart of the one that you most admire
To be tangled in love is like being twisted in barbwire
Your mate may be truthful, or a bold faced liar

Hate is a journey that would take you to hell's gate
Thieves, murderers, rapists should not be put up with at any rate
Once you get involved, changing your mind would be too late
Be careful, this kind of behavior is not considered great

Happiness is to be solid and strong with a sound mind
These attributes in a person are hard to find
But easily spotted because they are radiant, sweet, and kind
This situation will always leave you feeling and looking fine

Sadness is a state of mind that is easily defined
The expression on the face always gives the first sign
Some suffer from it for a long period of time
When it should be a temporary state of mind

In order to reach the height of a king
You should not settle for just anything
Life is like a boxer in a ring
So stand for something and do not fall for anything

Stand: Set a course for a particular destination.

1 Corinthians 16:13   "Watch ye, _**stand**_ fast in the faith, quit you like men, be strong,"

A BRUSH WITH DEATH

I had a brush with death so many times
It was not until 1995
That I really came alive
In March of that year, I nearly lost my mind

I went through several doctors
And did not respond to any of their diagnoses
Until this particular day I accidentally found one
She fitted the profile and the search was done

From that point on, life was not so blurred
The treatment help, she was a great referral
She and I was a match for one another
I retained her and stopped seeing the others

From that day on when I got sick
I always check the credentials of the doctors that I pick
When sickness hits, it can be a gravely lick
But when death touches you, life ends quick

I learned to deal with things and don't complain
Because I don't want to walk around acting insane
I see her monthly and my visits are not in vain
If I had to do it again, everything would be done the same

If you want to know who she is and where she lives,
You would address her as Doc, but not by her name
Depression is diffidently no joke and not a game
It can happen to anyone and you would never know how or when

Iniquities: Grossly immoral acts.

Isaiah 53:5   "But he *was* wounded for our transgressions, *he was* bruised for our ***iniquities***: the chastisement of our peace *was* upon him; and with his stripes we are healed."

WHICH WAY

The octagon red and white sign and red light indicates stop
The perfect round green light means go
The yellow, do not stop or go, but proceed at a pace that's slow
All of these signs determine the traffics flow
As we live, there are choices that comes with each day
In making decisions, should we choose our way or God's way?

We know all the laws and the rules
Yet, the divine lessons is what we should use
We learn to dot all "I" and cross every "t"
But, still make mistakes on things that we are unable to see
There is a new lesson that surfaces each day
Should we learn it our way or God's way?

In this life, we will go through trials and tribulations
Sometimes our stiff necks causes us to do hard labor
Life does not come with blue prints or instruction
But, if we follow the sixty-six books of the Bible
Our lives will be an increase instead of a deduction
So, should we follow our way or God's way?

In this world, life has it ups and it downs
We were born kings and queens, but without crowns
When we get to high; something causes us to fall down
The wrong turn can move us faster than a merry-go-round
Which leaves us breathless, not knowing what to say
Some obstacles we could have avoided had we chosen God's way

Way: A particular journey or the route followed or to be followed.

John 14:6   "Jesus saith unto him, I am they _way_, the truth, and the life: no man cometh unto the Father, but by me."

A SINNER'S CRY

Does God hears a sinner's cry?
Sure! As long as he repents before he dies
But, once he commits himself, he is forbidden to lie
If he does, a second chance at life will pass him by
Yes, God does hear a sinner's cry

There is joy in the presence of the Lord
It goes on to say a certain man had two sons
The devil was in the youngest one
He asked for his portion of goods
And headed off alone through the woods

Wasted his substance with riotous living
Ended with nothing because of his generous giving
He returned back to his native land
His father received him with open hands
The brother looked down at him as a worthless man

He was once lost and now is found
His father gave him a second chance around
The moment he returned home safe and sound
He chose to live and not die
God heard loud and clear this sinner's cry

Sinner: Somebody who commits a sin or who habitually does wrong.

Matthew 9:13   "But go ye and learn what *that* meaneth, I WILL HAVE MERCEY, AND NOT SACRIFICE: for I am not come to the righteous, but ___sinners___ to repentance."

BLIND MAN

There once was a man that was blind
He could not see from the front, side, or behind
But, he praised God with a pure heart and a sound mind
His sight was lost; but soon to be found

Acknowledging God made him a winner
His once thick lens soon became thinner
Positive changes in his sight came when he surrender
And brought him out of that dark cold world of a sinner

He opened his eyes and was able to see
He said, God has given a second chance to me
Now, I am ready to become what God wants me to be
His new eyes made him happy and free

Blind: Unwilling or unable to understand something.

Matthew 11:5 "The ***blind*** receive their sight, and the lame walk, the lepers are cleansed and the deaf hear, the dead are raised up, and the poor have the gospel preached to them."

ATTITUDE

Look! This is what happens when you have an attitude
You are out of control and act rather rude
Your face takes on a different shape and your mouth protrudes
If you think that this action, is portrayed only by dudes
Keep listening; you are about to become schooled

It is a laugh turned inside out
It takes you through life around and about
Your mind is not balanced because you are always in doubt
Can't hear anyone because all you do is shout
Because your disposition takes you the opposite route

It is a smile turned upside down
Juggling and jiggling like a circus clown
Transformed your face into a permanent frown
Crossing your speech between words and growls
Unable to tell if you are a person, dog, or an owl

Attitude is a thing that can affect anyone
A stranger, friend, mother, father, daughter, or son
We need to deal with our problems everyday
Because this action is a sickness and it blocks our way
Correcting this behavior can help save the day

Attitude: A position of the body proper to or implying an action or mental state.

Ephesians 6:4 "Fathers, do not provoke your children to **_anger_**, but bring them up in the discipline and instruction of the Lord."

CHOSEN ONE

We are all God's chosen children both daughters and sons
He fathered us all but favors certain ones
Some of them die as babies before their jobs begun
Others live to ripe old ages long after their work is done
Yet, it's a blessing to be God's chosen one

We live moment to moment each and everyday
Time should be special because God has the last say
Doctors were made to be licensed life- savers
Murders to be unlicensed life takers
But, God is still our only maker

He gives us breath so that we can breathe
Air is a gift, but we refuse to take heed
We were granted the power of knowledge so that we can read
But do we offer to help others by doing good deeds
That's why God chose certain ones to lead

God gave us everything and then some
Still most of us never overcome
We were placed here on earth to help one another and live
Some of us are so selfish; we just take and never give
God has his chosen ones, but life we can never relive

Chosen: Picked out from or preferred to the rest.

Matthew 22:14   "For many are called, but few *are <u>**chosen.**</u>*"

DEPRESSED

How does it feel to be depressed
Ask someone who has been consumed by stress
In this state of mind you no longer look your best
This is the beginning stage of a big and long test
To get through it you need therapy, medication, and rest

When you are depress, you settle for less
Important things you no longer remember so you take a wild guess
You answer all questions with a quick no or yes
Making it through each day with a prayer for success
Remembering what you choose to forget is a step towards progress

Re-living your life is such a dare
You try to take your life, because you don't care
Being successful the first time is very rare
The therapist counsel you but you can't hear
Knowing that all you have went through, leaves your heart bare

If you think being depress is something to boast about
Think again because it is not easy to snap out
So discuss your problems and clear all doubts
Never choose depression, instead try another route
Being a victim of this disease is nothing to joke about

Sick: An offensive term referring to somebody thoughts to have a psychiatric disorder that makes him or her dangerous to others…(or self).

James 5:14: "Is any ___sick___ among you? let him call for the elders of the church; and let them pray over him, anointing him with oil in the name of the Lord:"

SUICIDE

If you are tired of life and want an easy ride
Try a horse, a car, but not suicide
Anything that painful or bad you should never hide
It will eventually come out on the deadly side

Suicide is a dark mind deep within your mind
Ticking, waiting to explode in a matter of time
In this dark world, peace you cannot find
Thinking that you can destroy your life because it's yours, not mine

You attempted many times and you came close
Swallowing pills, hoping for an overdose
By the grace of God, you were saved that day
Simply because God heard you every-time that you pray

Remember when you said, thank you Lord for another day
Right then He allowed you more time and the right to stay
Allowing you to work life's situation in a different way
Preventing you from the final state that you would eternally lay

Suicide is never the easy way out
Life was granted to you and that's no doubt
Cry, plead, holler, dance, or shout
But never take the suicide route

Suicide: Somebody who deliberately kills himself or herself.

Matthew 27: 5 "And he cast down the pieces of silver in the temple, and departed, and went and ***hanged*** himself."

THIN LINE

Living is like walking through life on a thin line
Somewhere in between having sight and being blind
Things that we encounter are not always fine
But before they happen, we are always shown a sign
The signals are usually in front of us and rarely behind

We close our eyes and choose not to see
And say…as long as it is not affecting me
The journey is long especially for our sons
This is why most decide to give up before the age of twenty-one
Home becomes uncomfortable and they are always on the run

It is not easy to walk a thin line and definitely no fun
Only if we do the right things before the walks have begun
They get upset at the things their parents ask them to do
Not knowing one day they would be walking in their shoes
Wisdom is something that they would never lose

The walk in life is a very thin line
Some things should matter and others shouldn't mind
This way peace and love can easily be defined
Live each day as if it is yours and not mine
So, at the end of your walk, you can say that you did fine

Line: Useful information or an insight unto something.

Isaiah 28:13   "But the word of the LORD was unto them precept upon precept, precept upon precept; *line* upon *line*, *line* upon *line*; here a little, and there a little;"

BELIEVER

God gave His one and only begotten son
He worked six days and rested one
In the beginning, He created the Heavens and the Earth
He chose Moses to lead the Israelites to a new birth

We should not oppress one another
But, possess much love brother to brother
The Virgin Mary was Jesus' mother
Joseph was his Earthly Father

Some things are very hard to receive
The truth however, can easily be deceived
Hoping and praying, yet, words are great to conceive
But, the real meaning of life will prevail itself; only if we believe

Believer: Person who holds a particular belief.

Acts 5:14   "And ___believers___ were the more added to the Lord, multitudes both of men and women.)"

PURPOSE IN LIFE

My mother died just before I turned three
Which, was the beginning of her legacy
My purpose of life came to me at age forty-three
Writing poems is what it turned out to be
I write about things that I am able to see
This is why writing comes so easy to me

For forty-three years, I tried this and I tried that
Fighting for things that I have accepted and/or regret
Ventured here and there with no success
But, LORD knows I struggled to do my best
Not knowing this talent was in me since the day I was born
But, God manifested it when I became mentally grown

Everyone has a talent that is unique
It is presented to some and others have to seek
In life the seed that you sow is the one that you will reap
Some quickly reach their purpose and others have to creep
Getting there is the biggest leap
Once you arrive, you will become meek

Some learn what it is at an early age
Others, it takes years, even decades
If we don't recognize it, it can cause a rage
Reaching it, we have to go through a phase
But you would know when you get to that stage
Just be careful because your purpose can leave you in a daze

Purpose: The desire or the resolve necessary to accomplish a goal.

Proverbs 20:18   *"Every **purpose** is established by counsel: and with good advice make war."*

THE HAND THAT LIFE DEALT YOU

It's hard to figure out what life dealt you
A deck of cards can deal so many games
But, the hand that life dealt you has your name
No two lives are ever exactly the same
If you misjudge only you are the blame

The game of spade is different from blackjack
To win, you need spades in your stack
If you are dealt anything else, you are set back
The higher the spades, the better the bet
Playing someone else's hand, is something that you will regret

Take the game of craps
You can stand or squat but not sit
Stand when you make a bet
And squat when you collect
Proudly gather your winnings with no regrets

The easiest is the game of twenty-one
After dealing a few cards you are done
Who gets twenty-one or closes to it; won
It takes two or more cards, but never one
The hits in life that you take will leave you stun

Regardless what hand life deals you, play it
Take your hand and make the highest bid
To win, you must do whatever you have to do
Dealing with so many circumstances without a clue
But, it is the hand that life has dealt you

Hand: The influence or directing action of somebody or some.

Ecclesiastes 9:10   "Whatsoever thy ___hand___ findeth to do, do it with thy might:"

MAKING A STATEMENT

I want to change my hair color
Not black, brown, blonde, blue, but yellow
I want two holes in my ears
And I will have it pierced in a few days

I want a hole in my nose
And I will shop for my own clothes
The tattoo on my leg is a red rose
I wear rings on all ten of my toes

I have a gold ring on my bottom lip
I wear my pants sagging, over sized and below my hip
I am recognize by my fancy hair clip
A silver ball is in the back of my mouth and not on the tip

I listen to the music of my choice
Pumping up the bass and making a lot of noise
I love hip-hop, jazz, rock, and R&B
Be quiet parents, because I am in charge of me

Parents, controlling your teenagers can easily be done than said
Take control because you are responsible for how the bills are paid
In your household, parents, you are the head
Their changes came from friends, the TV, and the books that they have read

Trial: An instance of trouble or hardship.

2 Corinthians 8:2   "How that in a great ***trial*** of affliction the abundance
                         of their joy and their joy and their deep poverty
                         abounded unto the riches of their liberality."

HOW WELL DO CHILDREN LISTEN

When you talk to your children, it's like talking long distance
After a certain age, they create their own system
You can state clearly what you want them to do
But, they block out every word that comes from you

If you ask them to take out the trash
Their response, "I did it last"
If you ask them to water the grass or rake the yard
The subject changes to the crossing of the guards

When you ask them to vacuum the floor
Their friends always end up at the front door
By now you are fed up and say, "No more,"
Tension between you and them penetrates the air galore

As babies we have our children Christen
Always under parental supervision
With no exception for outside provision
So that they can live a godly mission

We can get our children to pay attention
By steering them in one direction without division
Live the life of a true Christian
Be a good example, eventually they will listen

Ears: The organ of hearing and balance in vertebrates that, in mammals, is divided into three parts, the external, middle, and inner ear.

Psalm 34:15 "The eyes of the LORD are upon the righteous, and his **_ears_** are open unto their cry."

MOTHER OF A TRICKSTER

I am your mother can't you see
The tricks that you pull, once belonged to me
Here is something you can learn from Mommy
Tricks start with a little wisdom and maturity

These things you call tricks that you pull
If you think for a moment that your kids will not pick it up; that's bull
Games like this would make you sick and full
Once the table turns, you must let go

The things that I see you do
You thought that you got away with it, did you?
Your offspring will copycat and call it fun
Before you continue, you better stop and listen to me son

A good mother teaches her children everything that they know
Truth and understanding they can always bestow
Something that I have to tell you and I would say it slow:
Living as a trickster is a part of life that you must let go

Mother: A woman who has raised a child, given birth to a child.

Acts 1:14 "These all continued with one accord in prayer and supplication, with the women, and Mary the ***mother*** of Jesus, and with his brethren."

WELL DONE

When you have done all that there is to do
Hold your head up, forget man, it's between God and you
When your family was down, you helped them up
Now that you need them, they are taking you around and about
But, what goes around comes around, and that's no doubt
When they need you again, don't deviate, take the same route

In church you worship in total faith
From the members you received pure hate
But you should never change at any rate
They will answer to God before it's too late
That's why we are responsible for our own fate
Your job is not done until you enter heaven or hell's gate

In school, students walk around acting so kool
But when they get in trouble they look like fools
The mean things that they do, they call it fun
Actually this is how real trouble begun
Too late to correct, you have been caught
Now, deal with the consequences that your actions bought

Listen! If an adult chastises you
Be thankful, because it is the right thing to do
So the next time you think about acting up in school
Remember to use the lessons as a learning tool
You waste precious time, whenever you acted the fool
Stop! Spare yourself of the judge's rule

Life is an individual job forced on you
Something that was not asked for, so what can you do?
Dealing with it day by day, thinking that you are on the roll
Through trials and tribulations, life still takes its toll
But, you must continue to roll and pace the run
When the race is over, God will say, "Well done" my servant "Well Done"

Well: To surge from within or grow stronger so as to threaten to burst forth.

Matthew 25: 21 "His lord said unto him, **_Well_** done, thou good and faithful servant: thou hast been faithful over a few things, I will make thee ruler over many things: enter thou into the joy of thy lord."

HE GIVES YOU BUSINESS OF YOUR OWN

Be careful not to engage in other's affairs
People situations cause you a great deal of wear and tear
The hustle and scuffle creates a big scare
For you to come out as being innocent is very rare
So when you think that you have solved the problem please beware
Soon the table will turn on you my dear

You should never throw sticks and stones
Eventually God will give you some business of your own
Being too concerned about how others do things
Living day by day fearing death's sting
If you live in a glass house you should never throw rocks
Because you are not safe not even under keys and locks

The battle is not yours to fight
When it comes to others' problems, you…take a flight
Because the outcome for you is not always a beautiful sight
So listen to me and do what is right
And don't act like you know it all and are too grown
God has a way of giving you some business of your own

Own: To acknowledge full personal responsibility for something.

James 1:22   "But be ye doers of the word, and not hearers only, deceiving your _**own**_ selves.

CONDITION OF A MAN

Every creature on earth God created, but he formed man
He has given a heaven for them all except man
Foxes have holes and the birds have nests
But, man has nowhere to lay his head

Man can have the most comfortable bed
Yet, sometimes he has no place to lay his head
He has the capability to become anything
But, chooses to sit around to see what life brings

He was given a voice so that he can be heard
But when it comes to putting it in action, he is quieter than a bird
Every man is given a talent to do at least one thing
Some would sit on their talents and do nothing

All of life's wounds they are able to heal
Because man is so unfocused, he misses out on the deal
Not realizing that God gives him the strength to do all things
Still, he sits around day after day to see what life brings

God created this earth to be an earthly heaven for you and me
But we choose to live by worrying about things we cannot see
He gave a home to the foxes, and the bees
But man he gave him the opportunity to be free

Never feel sorry about the condition of a man
America is one of the world's richest land
Life little glitches, man should be able to withstand
Because the situation he is in was created by his own hand

Adam: In the Bible, the first man, created by God.

Genesis 5:1 "This is the book of the generations of ***Adam***. In the day God created man, in the likeness of God made he him;"

SEASONAL FRIEND

When I first met Mrs. Short
Her smile was tighter than a knot
As I talked to her, while I standing on my lot
We developed a friendship from the conversation we sought

We first met not knowing one another
Soon learned that divine spirit bought us together
God said, we did not need to know each other
His plans that He has for us, no man can asunder

He has unexplained events no one can see
Yes, we may guess, but the true answer does not come from you or me
Remember who God is and let it be
He has the last word for you and me

It took me a week to learn the routine
I knew not to disturb you until after ten
Sunshine or rain, I refuse to bend
I will respect you as a seasonal friend

Spending hours on the computer day and night
Time was whining down and research was tight
You stayed focused and did not lose sight
But, when I did see you, you were all right

I limited the time that I spend
With my seasonal friend
Meeting new people is of essence
And I will do it again and again

Friend: Somebody who has a close personal relationship of mutual affection and trust with another.

John 15:14 "Ye are my _**friends**_, if ye do whatsoever I command you."

THE REVEREND DR. MARTIN LUTHER KING

January 15th does this date have a ring?
Sure, it's the birthday of Dr. Martin Luther King
He was a Leader as well as a preacher
He was considered to be a great teacher
Most of all, he was a wonderful leader

He led marches from city to city without fear
Marching for desegregation, he was always in front, never in the rear
He spoke morbidly, yet never shared a tear
Shot down by an assassin's bullet as the crowd sadly stared
But not once he feared death nor was he scared

King was the man that everyone wanted to be
He marched boldly and faithfully for the world to see
On a warm spring day, a whooping eighty degrees
His life was taken, it was a sad day for everyone to include me
But, the death of this leader, helped set us free

The third Monday in January does have a ring
This is the time that we march and sing
Walking hand and hand, oh what joy it brings
People from all nations, joined together
Celebrating the memory of The Reverend Dr. M.L. King

King: The principal man or preeminent male figure in a specific field.

Luke 19:38 "Saying, BLESSED BE THE *KING* THAT COMETH IN THE NAME OF THE LORD: peace in heaven, and glory in the highest."

SLEEP

Now, I lay me down to sleep
Pleasant memories, I pray will keep
Everything that I sow, I will surely reap

As I close my room door
Bad dreams, I hope no more
This path, I crossed many times before

Whatever I did or say this very day
Means nothing, regardless how hard I pray
Because my Master has the last say

As I lift up my voice high in Praise
It leaves me limp and in a daze
Life's journey is like walking through a maze

Enjoy your life each and everyday
Because it is not here to stay
It will eventually pass and go away

Time is short on earth and we know it
As tall as we stand, as low as we sit
Live life to the fullest and never quit

Sleep: A state of partial or full unconsciousness.

Proverbs 3:24   "When thou liest down, thou shall not be afraid: yea, thou
                    shalt lie down, and thy ***sleep*** shall be sweet."

LIFE

Life will turn a smile into a frown
It ups and downs will knock you to the ground
It will leave you spinning around and around
Before you know it, you are down

You are promised three scores and ten
Yet, some have not started living not even then
But, you have to deal with whatever life sends
And some things in life will make you bend

You do good and bad things and make them blend
But, life cannot be borrowed or lend
Your life is yours, you cannot give it to a friend
You must strive to endure it unto the end

Immortality: Eternal life or the ability to live forever.

1 Corinthians 15:53   "For the corruptible must put on incorruption, and this mortal *must* put on ***immortality***."

HAPPINESS

Happiness is a thing if not careful, it stays domain
Trapped inside or comes out as pain
Sometimes it may take a whiff of fresh air
But, it never comes out in the light
Because it does not want to be seen
Therefore, inside of you happiness remains

Happiness cannot be bought or taught
It is something that is individually learned
It has no special direction or destination
But, it does travel for miles and miles
It travels both short and long distances
And it always get where it wants to go

Happiness has two sides, the inside and the outside
It has a timer that can be turned on and off
It operates both day and night
It is capable of crying and smiling
Yes, it can be very be-wildering
Happiness, when it comes out; oh what a beautiful sight

Happy: Resulting in something pleasant or welcome.

John 5:11   "Behold, we count them ___*happy*___ which endure. Ye have heard of the patience of Job, and have seen the end of the Lord; that the Lord is very pitiful, and of tender mercy."

CREATION

God created the skies and the seas
He made flowers for the bees
To make honey and nectar
For the people near and afar

First, He created the heaven and the earth
Without form, void, and before the first birth
Then came darkness and light, such a beautiful sight
He named it day and night

He formed the firmament in such a way
Named it Heaven before he prayed
Came up with evening and morning on the second day
Under this Heaven, dry land came into play

He called the dry land earth and the waters seas
This bought forth grass and fruit trees
The darkness and light was for a good reason
Days and nights, together they created the four seasons

God knew that these were good features
But, He knew that the world needed living creatures
He made two of each kind, male and female
Now, life formation were beginning to look real

God made man from the dust of the ground
Looked for his soul mate, but she was no where around
He then took the man's rib and made a woman perfectly sound
The earth was perfect until they ate the fruit
and their differences were found

Create: Bring something into existence.

Genesis 1:1   "In the beginning God ***created*** the heaven and the earth."

CHURCH PEOPLE

Living a good Christian life is what we want others to see
Living right is the way God wants us to be
We try praying and fasting everyday
But, these two things are God's way
Thinking that one religion is better than the other
Believe it or not, what matters is what we do and say to one another

Little that we know, the answer comes from Our Father
We ask our birth father for forgiveness for some things
But, only our Heavenly Father can forgive us from our sins
The line between good and bad is very thin
HE understands all our body languages to include a smile or a grin
If you break your communication with God you will never win

Church People cannot choose for you heaven or earth
This you get from your Heavenly Father before your birth
Only you can make that choice of heaven or hell
If you listen to Church People, oh well!
Free your soul or keep it locked-up in a cell
On judgment day, how you lived your life will surely tell

Christian: Relating to Christianity, or belonging to or maintained by a christian organization, especially a church.

1 Peter 4:16 "Yet if *any man suffer* as a ***Christian***, let him not be ashamed; but let him glorify God on this behalf."

ENEMY

Enemy is a person that's within me
Created a world that should not be
Presented a situation for me to see
Practiced hatred and is very ungratefully

An opponent that tries to attack
Rather if I am on my feet or on my back
It is worse than a fatal heart attack
Can care less about how I feel or react

It makes my life harder than a brick
Knocks me down with just one lick
Twirl me around as if I was a stick
And will mess me up, rather fast and quick

My enemy started out as a friend
Someone that's hard to trust again
Be careful, because my enemy became my best friend
Because it rode my back to the end

Enemy: An individual or a group that is seen as forcefully adverse or threatening.

Matthew 5:44 "But I say unto you, Love your ___enemies,___ bless them that curse you, do good to them that hate you, and pray for them which despitefully use you, and persecute you;"

DEVIL

A devil is an angel in disguise
More apt to be easily recognize
Simply by a direct look into his eyes
If you encounter one, stand up and rise
His actions will leave you surprise

A devil comes in more than one form
Sometimes quiet and other times like a storm
Regardless if he dresses plain or in uniform
He is never stationary because he loves to roam
Yes, he knocks from door to door, home to home

A devil may do good and bad deeds
In effort to get you to become his seed
Always beware and take heed
Because the devil is full of greed
He will enter your soul and take the lead

Devil: An evil spirit, particularly a subordinate of Satan.

Revelation 12:9   "And the great dragon was cast out, that old serpent, called the ___Devil___, and Satan, which deceiveth the whole world: he was cast out into the earth, and his angels were cast out with him."

ORDER OUR STEPS

One, two, three, four, life will shut your door
But, God will open it and that's for sure
Some people are born into fame, other have to play the game
Once God touches our lives, we are never the same

As long as we live, problems will arise
Trouble touches all of us regardless of our size
Sometimes it remains even after our demised
Whatever the end brings, at least we tried

God comes into all of our lives
He controls it and that's no jive
Our names are always in His Archive
Yes, He is the One that keeps us alive

Moses was a man controlled by God
Do you remember the story of Moses and the Rod
Like Moses, we must be on one accord
Because our steps are ordered by the Lord

Ordered: An instruction to do something.

Psalm 37:23   "The steps of a good man are ***ordered*** by the LORD: and he delighteth in his way."

THIS HOUSE

This house is every man's dream
Built on a promise that can be seen
Use of hard structure and solid beams
It cause the lives of many trees

First, they had to clear the land
Some used tools, others use their bare hands
The work was done by both machines and man
To complete the job, they did everything that they can

To build this house they also had to remove tons of sand
Sweating profusely without a moment to fan
To complete this house would be grand
This house was built by man, but on God's land

House: A building made for people to live in.

Proverbs 24:3   "Through wisdom is an **_house_** builded; and by understanding
                    it is established:"

TOMORROW

Tomorrow is a day that will never come
But, it is always the next day to come
It is a day that we will never see
Is tomorrow even the next day

Tomorrow is in the future
So far, we cannot imagine it
Something to come, yet so far away
It is a promised infinite day

Tomorrow means on the day after today
This explanation does not clearly explains
Today means on or for this day
So, what is tomorrow? Will it ever come?

Tomorrow: In the future the day after today.

Matthew 6:34   "Take therefore no thought for ***the morrow***: for ***the morrow*** shall take thought for the things of itself. Sufficient unto the day is the evil thereof."

WHO ARE YOU

Who are you; are you the person you claim to be
Or are you a naked frame that eyes cannot see
Who you are lies within your heart
This is a true value that would never part

Are you the person that they say you are?
The truth is: No, not by far
The true you are hidden inside
Only you know where it hides

It was said that you would not amount to anything
Be all that you can and see what life brings
The mind is a terrible thing to waste
You are very unique and have good taste

So, who are you, you are who God created you to be
Well pronounced, so that the world can clearly see
The true you is reveal, that's what set you free
Getting and staying in touch with your spirit man is the key

Soul: The spiritual part of a human being that is believed to continue to exist after The body dies.

Genesis 2:7 "And the LORD God formed man *of* the dust of the ground, and breathed into his nostrils the breath of life: and man became a living ***soul***."

BORN

Does it matter where you were born?
You will find the answer once you leave home
Your niche began the day that you were born
Your glitch start the day that you became grown

You have an idea where you came from
Because you were told by someone
But, have no concept where you are going
Because no one has the answer to that one

You were born for a reason
Life has its purpose just like the four seasons
Nature changes each time one comes
The same happens to all of us not just some

So, does it matters where you were born
Sometimes it does and sometimes it doesn't
It cannot be determine if you have no voice
But, as long as you are able to talk, you have a choice

Born: Given a particular status or condition by or at birth.

1 John 5:4   "For whatsoever is ***born*** of God overcometh the world: and this is the victory that overcometh the world, even our faith."

OUR FATHER

Our father which art in heaven, hallowed be thy name
The Father, the Son, and the Holy Ghost are one of the same

Thy kingdom come, His will; will be done on earth and in heaven
He has the power to call us home at any time, twenty-four/seven

I always pray, "Give us this day our daily bread"
After life is over, I know I have a resting-place to lay my head

Forgive us our debts, as we forgive our debtors
God equally loves the victims as well as the perpetrators

Lead us not into temptation, but deliver us from evil
Our spiritual instinct is the factor that separates us from non-believers

God is the kingdom, the power, and the glory, forever
He separates us by our love for him and not by our gender

Father: A male parent of a child.

1 John 5:7   "For there are three that bear record in heaven, the ***Father***, the
Word, and the Holy Ghost: and these three are one."

HOW DARE DO YOU BE DIFFERENT

(Remembrance of Columbine)

We all were born of a woman
Equal contribution of a man
Living daily from mouth to hand
Life, we never fully understand
Each day we struggle to do the best that we can
But, how dare do we be different

Some of us are tall
Others are either medium or small
To be conceived was not our choice at all
Majority of us are poor, which is a downfall
Minority is in royalty; they made a good call

One was black; the other eleven were white
But, they all were equal in God's eyesight
Though we look at each other with limited light
Not able to explain, we chose to fight
Through the eyes of a man we try to do what is right
When we all just want to make it through another night

The color of our skin is one of the same
Those that came out of this alive must have felt some kind of fame
No, they are just purely blessed that God did not call their names

It is sad that we do not understand each other
Instead, we fight, curse, hate, and kill our own brother
To get to know one another, we do not bother
We rather dwell in our sorrows and sober

The blessing is in this day; we cannot depend on tomorrow
For the twelve fatal victims in Littleton Co., a smile cannot be borrowed
Their friends, classmates, and families are left behind in total horror
We thought that the pain was harder on their mothers
No, equal tears were shared by their fathers

Authorities checked the school ground
But, the perpetrators schemes were perfectly planned and sound
Prior to the plan, they checked the school all around
They video outside the school's property bound
And two weeks later more bombs were found

We don't have to act like kissing brothers, sisters, cousins, or lovers
In these time and days, we need to get to know one another
So this ordeal would not be copycatted again, in the same place or any other

We all are descendents of Adam and Eve
Rather we choose to know, care, or believe
We are one generation extended from one rod
Little that we all know, it started with God

Remember! He gave His one and only begotten Son
With the intent that we live in this world as one
So, how dare do we be different?

Remembrance: A retained mental impression; memory.

1 Corinthians 11:24   "And when he had given thanks, he brake it, and said, Take eat, this is my body, which is broken for you: this do in ***remembrance*** of me."

IF I

You are not responsible for how people treat you
But, you are liable for how you react
We always say what we will or will not do
If we were in someone else's shoe

The answer always comes after the test
In real situations we do not think our best
Because it is hard in the midst of stress
We react without taking a second guess

People often say, "If I were you, I would!"
The majority of us say, "You should"
All the time you are saying, "I wish I could,"
Remember you are responsible for yourself
and that should be well understood

If: A conjunction used to indicate the circumstances that would have to exist in order for an event to happen.

John 15:7   "*If* ye abide in me, and my words abide in you, ye shall ask what ye will, And it shall be done unto you."

BELIEVES

God gave His one and only begotten son
He worked six days and rested one
In the beginning, He created the Heavens and the Earth
He chose Moses to lead the people of Israel to a new birth

We should not oppress one another
But possess much love for our brother
The Virgin Mary was Jesus' mother
Joseph was his Earthly Father
Yet, he was God's only son
And this is how the story begun

Some things that are said are hard to receive
The truth can easily be deceived
Lies after lies that cannot be reprieve
Hoping and praying, the truth is hard to conceive
But, the truth will prevail itself only if we believe

Believe: To accept that something is true or real.

Job 9:16   "If I had called, and he had answered me; yet would I not _**believe**_ that he had hearkened unto my voice."

STARTING OVER

If you think that starting life all over is going to be fun
Just the thought of it, makes you want to run
The smallest details is hotter than the sun
It makes you wonder, how do I begun?

Memories of your earlier age, you would have to be fed
Coming from someone else, you can falsely be led
Writing the truth is like bumping heads
Questioning each word every time it is read

Birth to the age of two, someone did everything for you
From combing your hair to tying your shoes
At three you were still too young to remember and see
Yet, you were almost there at age of four
Five you were able to understand a little more
School age, living life through a different door

Life is no longer the way it use to be
You are out of your comfort zone you see
Now reserve and not feeling so free
Starting over is not easy, not even for me
Life is tough, don't you agree

Beginning: The first part or early stages of something.

John 1:1   "In the ***beginning*** was the Word, and the Word was with God, and the Word was God."

DRUGS

Drugs are serious and it's not a game
By any other name, the result is still the same
It does not matter rather you are a child, adult, man or a dame
Once you try it, your life would never be the same

Some comes in a form of a rock
One hit and you are lock
Regardless if you are a visitor or a member of the block
Wherever you land, consider yourself docked

Rich, homely or lonely, the dealer says "the first hit is on me"
For he knows what you would soon come to be
Turns your life so dark and blind, leaving you unable to see
Now, who's the blame; the dealer; no, yet the first hit is free

So powerful and comes in so many forms
Despite, how you consumed it, it always causes a storm
Rather you are a Lawyer, doctor, or whoever, it causes you to roam
Leaving you broke strung out, confused, and all alone

Drugs: A chemical substance that has known biological effects on humans.

Galatians 5:20   "Idolatry, witchcraft, hatred, variance, emulations, wrath, strife, **_seditions_**, hereles."

AGE IS ONLY A NUMBER

What is age; it is only a number
If you do not believe it put a sixty and a thirty
Year old together and watch them rumble

The sixty year old has so much spunk
He dear not stumble
To him, age is just only a number

He goes through his daily routine as if he is thirty
Up early running around fulfilling his agenda
Keeping up with the thirty year old and never slumber

Thirty year old tries to do everything he does and fumbles
But, he is less as sharp and not so humble
Now we see why age is only a number

Age: The length of time that somebody or something has existed.

Exodus 7:7   "And Moses was ***fourscore years old***, and Aaron ***fourscore and three years old***, when they spake unto Pharaoh."

DRIVING

Driving can be a lot of fun
Despite, being under the age of twenty-one
The law, is for both your daughters and sons
The stage in which the fun of life has just begun

At age sixteen, they get their permits
It is not a license, nor is it permanent
Not a toy, nor is it a free ride
A licensed person must be by their side

At age eighteen, they get a little lead way
But, they can drive only during the day
Don't get caught driving at night
Because the police radar has you in its sight

At twenty-one they are home free
Now, they are legal according to the DMV
Able to drive all day and all night
And can care less if the policeman is in sight

Driving: Having the ability or influence to make something new or different happen.

Deuteronomy 28:37 "And thou shalt become an astonishment, a proverb, and a byword, among all nations whither the LORD shall **_lead_** thee."

MAN WITH A PLAN

A man cannot succeed unless he has a plan
His best instruments are his mind and his hands
His long term goal is like tilting land
A slight cross between dirt and sand
The outcome is what will make the man

A man will face past, present and future problems
That he has seen, is not ready for, or willing to see
But has to deal with them, whatever they maybe
No pain, no gain, life will test you over and over again
Without a plan, you are not thinking like a man

For a man to succeed, he needs a plan
So he can stand tall and be a real man
He can conquer the world on what he knows
With a plan he has an idea where he wants to go
He can even go places where he has never been before

Man: An adult male human being.

Job 1:1 "There was a man in the land of UZ, whose name was Job; and that ___man___ was perfect and upright, and one that feared God, and eschewed evil."

AMERICA

America is name the land of plenty
Yet, it is other countries enemy
It is the dream of everyone
To come here to America

In America you have opportunities galore
The freedom here helps to open many doors
It can take you where man has never been before
Also, it closes as well as it opens doors

There is a lot here for you to see
And it is up for grabs for both you and me
We can obtain it without being on bending knees
Opportunities are there and semi free

America reaches out to its enemies
Counties both far and abroad
Despite, written treaties
And written or spoken words

America is the place to be
Spend a few days in undeveloped countries
From this experience, you will agree
That America is the place that will set you free

Plenty: An adequate or more than adequate amount or quantity.

Genesis 41:29   "Behold, there come seven years of great ***plenty*** throughout all the land of Egypt."

OUR STEPS ARE ORDERED

One, two, three, four, life will shut your door
But, God will open it and that's for sure
Some people are born into fame, others have to play the game
Once God touches our lives, we are never the same

As long as we live, problems will arise
And it often takes us by surprise
Trouble touches all of us regardless of our size
Sometimes it remains even after our demise

God comes into all of our lives
He controls it and that's no jive
It does not matter how we thrive
Our names are always in His Archive

In the Book of Exodus Moses was controlled by God
Do you remember the story of Moses and the rod
To serve God, we must be on one accord
Because all of our steps are ordered by the Lord

Steps: Short movement made by raising one foot and lowering it ahead of the other foot.

2 Samuel 22:37 "Thou hast enlarged my ***steps*** under me; so that m feet did not slip."

WHEN I CRY

When I cry it is usually at night
Making sure that I am out of everyone's sight
I don't cry only when the sky is bright
Holding back the tears is such a fight

When I cry, tears fill my eyes
Thick as a heavy rain falling from the skies
Trouble come my way bye and bye
The pressure makes me feel like I have died

When I cry over things, big or small
Problems always build a wall
But, I have to answer to the call
Built-up pressure makes me fall

When I cry, Life passes me bye
Can't see clearly for the water in my eyes
Dealing with problems is hard, no lie
But, my burdens are lifted when I cry

Cry: To shed tears as the result of a strongly felt emotion.

Proverbs 21:13 "Whoso stopped his ears at the _**cry**_ of the poor, he also shall _**cry**_ himself, but shall not be heard."

GOOD-BYE

Good-bye is a word that would make you cry
The thought will leave your eyes dry
The pain is sharper than a thorn in your side
From just the word of someone saying good-bye

A pleasant hello soon becomes a sad good-bye
These tears will last for years
Get a hold of yourself, as sad as it may be
The signs were there, but you failed to see

A short good-bye is like a long hello
Both can leave you feeling very low
But, it leaves a seed for you to sow
In a solid relationship both parties will grow

Good-bye: A concluding remark or gesture of parting.

Ezekiel 21:21   "For the king of Babylon stood at the ***parting*** of the way, at the head of the two ways, to use divination:"

FROWN

A frown is a smile turn upside down
It makes you look like a silly clown
It's heavier than a kings's crown

It wrinkles the forehead
Makes your eyes feel like lead
Puts bad thoughts in your head

To others, you look bad
Because your expression is sad
The look on your face can easily be read

You can turn a smile into a frown
Just turn the smile upside down
Smile! Turn that frown around

Laugh: To express amusement.

Ecclesiastes 3:4   "A time to weep, and a time to ***laugh***; a time to mourn, and a time to dance;"

INTELLIGENCE verses IGNORANCE

Intelligence is a niche in the brain stem
Ignorance is a glitch and you are the blame
Intelligence keeps you ahead of the game
Ignorance makes you feel so ashamed
No, they are not one of the same

Intelligence you are consider to be bright
You try real hard with all of your might
Everything that you touch seems to come to light
With a mind like this you will be alright

Ignorance comes with a different price
Even if you try with all of your might
Decisions that you make would never be sound and tight
Because life for you will always be a fight

Ignorance and aptitude, together they do not go
You are more likely to end up at the welfare's door
Intelligence is the way to go for sure
It will open up doors galore

Ways: A method, style, or manner of doing something.

Ezekiel 18:29   "Yet saith the house of Israel, The way of the Lord is not equal? are not your _ways_ unequal?"

RELATIONSHIP

A relationship is serious and it's not a game
Like building a house, you must have a frame
Things that do not fit regroup and try again
It's like using a nail to seal a window pane
Hoping that it would go straight through and not bend

Communication is certainly not a crime
Build it up, one conversation at a time
It's like placing the shingles on the roof
Making sure that they are secure and rain proof

Love is like building a perfect deck
Of course it replaces the porch, but what the heck
Each joint must be connected at the neck
To prevent a disastrous wreck

Building a relationship is like furniture in a house
It always takes two equally dedicated people, no doubt
An unequal yoke can turn a relationship inside out
True Commitment to each other is what it is all about

Commit: To put into charge or trust.

Job 5:8   "I would seek unto God, and unto God would I ___*commit*___ my cause:"

CHANGE

When I change and become the real me
I become so transparent, yet I could clearly see
Strangers in my life they soon to be
They began to look at me differently
I am still the same to a certain degree
Much more assertive and feel so free

To them the glass looks half full
Confused, checking me from head to toe
I am now where I always wanted to go
The journey was very long and slow
But, I finally opened that closed door

Now, people look at me through both eyes
Because I am no longer in my disguise
Finally free, oh how I have arise
That person I use to be is now demise
Free as a bird, I can fly as high as the skies

Change: To make radical difference.

Hosea 4:7 "As they were increased, so they sinned against me: therefore will I ***change*** their glory into shame."

DECISIONS

In life you will have your ups and downs
But, it is up to you to turn it around
Other folks' opinions are good and sound
When trouble comes, they are nowhere to be found

In life you have to make certain decisions
And it will cause both minor and major divisions
That's okay, as long as you know who you are
Don't depend on others choices, their opinions are afar

Making decisions is something that you have to do
Which, it should be made only by you
People think that they can fit into your shoe
But, they have their own problems too

Life's decisions is like wearing a crown
You can wear it with a smile or a frown
Yes, you will have more ups than downs
Don't forget, problem solving will always be around

Decision: Act or process of deciding.

Joel 3:14   "Multitudes, multitudes in the valley of ***decision***: for the day of the LORD is near in the valley of ***decision***."

A WISE MAN

A wise man needs no audience or fans
He will do the best that he can
And knows exactly which way to go
Rather, he moves fast or takes it slow

A wise man leaves home alone
Usually, before he is fully grown
He moves from city to city
Before you know it, he is long gone

A wise man has his journey well mapped
Works hard, but knows when to nap
He travels very far and long
And travels very light and alone

A wise man always has two or more plans
Knows exactly how and where he will land
He just does the best that he can
This is what makes him a wise man

Wise: Having or showing wisdom or knowledge usually from learning or experience.

Hosea 14:9   "Who is *wise*, and he shall understand these things? Prudent, and he shall know them? For the ways of the LORD are right, and the just shall walk in them: but the transgressors shall fall therein."

GOOD NIGHT

Good night, sleep tight
It has been a long day
So, I guess. I would call it a night

I am going to get my beauty rest
So that I can get up in the morning fresh
This new day will require my very best

It is filled with many requests
Without sleep, I have to take a guess
I would like to do better and not less

So, I will sleep comfortably tonight
Get up in the morning all bubbling and bright
Thank God for this day, I will do what's right

Good:　　　　Of high quality.

Joshua 1:6　　"Be strong and of a ***good*** courage:"

LAUGH OR CRY

The same things that make us laugh
Are the same things that will make us cry
When we are born, people laugh
But, when we die, they cry

At ages one to seventeen, we do crazy things
From ages eighteen to twenty-one
We are surprise at what life brings
Twenty-two and on, life has a sting

It is not the crazy blues
But, it is from the choices that we choose
Some battles we win, others we lose
Both are the result of life's golden rules

When bad things happen, we cry
Good things, we usually laugh
Rather tears, a smile, or a frown
Whatever, we cannot turn life around

Before we know it, life will past us by
So, always wear more smiles than frowns
The same things that make us laugh
Are the same things will eventually make us cry

Wisdom: Ability to discern inner qualities and relationship.

1 Chronicles 22:12   "Only the LORD give thee ***wisdom*** and understanding.."

MEMORIES

Memories are something that we cannot see
It is an individual thing to both you and me
It is thoughts that will forever be
A lifelong thing that will never set us free

Some of these things, we will repeat
Regardless what problem it may create
Sure, they are in our heads
As vibrant as usual, they are not dead

All memories were not caused by words
Some were caused from physical actions
Others came from verbal abuse
However, they all have their own use

It controls the things that we do
Rather good or bad, it changes you
This is a situation that we cannot undo
Because its bond is tighter than super glue

Memories will be with us as long as we live
Some comes free, others with a price
If they are pleasant, it can be nice
If bad, it may cost you a little sacrifice

Know: To have learned.

Job 28:13   "Man **_knoweth_** not the price thereof; neither is it found in the land of the living."

IN TIMES OF SORROW

In times of sorrow
What can I say?
Or what can I do?
To be true to you

Words are no big deal
Money does not make it heal
Love you cannot not feel
To you, nothing seems to be real

My thoughts are with you
My prayers are too
In addition to these two
I am here for you

Friends, come in few
To be there and comfort you
A true friend indeed
Is all that you will ever need

In times of sorrow
Always do your best
Pray and count it as a test
Because God will do the rest

Sorrow: A feeling of deep distress caused by loss, disappointment, or other misfortune suffering by oneself or others.

Ecclesiastes 1:18 "For in much wisdom is much grief: and he that increaseth knowledge increaseth ***sorrow***."

GOOD OLE DAYS

I can remember the good ole days
Crimes were rare and we had no fears
We knew all of our neighbors and cared
We left the doors unlocked and were not scared

There were never any real fights
Except rarely on Friday nights
Partying hard to the music in the clubs bright lights
A few drinks helped them to express their rights

Materiel things were not important back in the day
Because no one had the money to pay
With the lack of materialistic things
Life were simpler then than it is today

Bread were ten cents a loaf
Purchased with a promissory note
A promise to pay at a later day
Most families shopped that way

Living can be much better today
If we live it like we did in the good ole day
With this dog eat dog world, what can we say
We can never bring back the good ole days

Living: Alive, not dead.

Lamentations 3:39   "Wherefore doth a **_living_** man complain, a man for the punishment of his sins?"

ON THE OUTSIDE LOOKING IN

It is funny how people judge you from the outside
They cannot see past the door or its frame
They choose one word and make it a sentence
Sentence then turns into a paragraph
Paragraph turns into a story
Finally, the story turns into a book

One word depicts one's entire life
Now it has a beginning, middle, and an ending
Judging someone can become detrimental
Sometimes it helps and sometimes it hurts
Both good and bad scars last forever
But, the impression can remain a lifetime

So, the next time you are on the outside looking in
Forget what you think because that's where rumors begin
It is based on opinions that did not come from within
Now, before you ruin someone's entire life
Simply because you were on the outside looking in
Think first because the results are never a win, win

Watch: A period of time spent observing something or someone closely.

Proverb 8:34 "Blessed is the man that heareth me, ***watching*** daily at my gates, waiting, at the posts of my doors."

TRUE FRIENDSHIP

When we first met, we promised it would be
A life long friendship between you and me
We were so close and the very best of friends
Promised that we will be this way until the end

Then again it is funny what life brings
When two people believe in the same things
Our love for each other bonds the link
To become one, we can careless what others think

Birds fly south only once a year
Same goes for hibernation of the bears
Nature provides and it might sound rare
Going against the norm, they don't dare

There is a time to be born an a time to die
A time to smile and a time to cry
A time to walk and a time to talk
These things will happen regardless of our daily walk

There are fall and spring
There are nights and days
There are summer and winter
These are all of the things that make us sing
Think about what true friendship brings

Friendship: A relationship between two or more people who are friends.

Proverbs 22:24 "Make no ___*friendship*___ with an angry man, and with a furious man thou shalt no go;"

PARANOID

People are usually fearful
To the point of no trust
Everything that they touch, they crush
To them, acting normal is consider a rush

They are always at their best
To the point of being obsessed
Low keyed compared to the rest
Dealing with others is always a test

People try to read their minds
Make judgments from their signs
Never know their true feelings inside
Because they will not allow any personal tides

Trusting, is a word that is wrought
Emanated from their subtle thoughts
Dealing with them, everyone tries to avoid
Naive of the disease called "Paranoid"

Fear: An unpleasant feeling of apprehension or distress.

Amos 3:8   "The lion hath roared, who will not _**fear**_? The Lord GOD hath spoken, who can but prophesy?"

A DEVIL AT EVERY LEVEL

We are supposed to be saved by grace
Questioned heavy by the human race
Everyone wants to meet Christ face to face
Then we would know that we are in the right place

We all want to enter at Heaven's gate
But, not mindful of what it takes
The right step takes us to another level
But, the higher the steps, the greater the devil

We live a good life, by doing what's right
Being a Christian, it is such a big fight
Dealing with others that are contrite
They say and do bad things just for spite

Christians pray for the world both day and night
In hope that sinners will see the light
The outcome is not always sunny and bright
Hoping that our fervent prayers will make everything alright

Getting there you will fight many devils
It's a rough road at each level
If you don't quit, you will win this race
Only if you stay in God's good grace

Devils: A mischievous, troublesome, or high-spirited people.

John 6:70 "Jesus answered them, Have not I chosen you twelve, and one of you is a ***devil***?"

HEAR MY CRY

Why doesn't anyone hear my cry
When I use their tissues to wipe my eyes
Noticeable, but they just pass me by
Regardless, how hard I try

Everyone sees my red eyes
Looked me right in the face and sigh
Still, they just passed on by
No, I would never ask why

Does anyone see my face
Swollen and sad with disgrace
A look that cannot be erase
A scenario of the worst case

Talking and no one recognizes my voice
Guess this disguise was a poor choice
Does anyone hear my cry
Yes, get over it and do the dance of rejoice

Hear: To understand fully by listening attentively.

Nahum 3:19   "There is no healing of thy bruise; thy wound is grievous: all
                 That _**hear**_ the bruit of thee shall clap the hands over thee:"

HALF GROWN ROSE

Life is like a half grown rose
Enjoying it day by day instead of scores
Things in life comes and goes
Smalls steps will get you there for sure

Being a half grown rose
You must deal with life blows
There will be highs as well as lows
Trouble will knock you to the floor

Life is like a bud of a rose
It opens and blooms as it grows
Eventually they both will come to a close
But not before their purpose of life is disclose

Careful, because life can be like a rose bud
Both life and a rose can be cloned
Your life's journey is yours and yours alone
Only when it has fully developed, but never half grown

Grown: Having developed and matured.

Ruth 1:13   "Would ye tarry for them till they were ***grown***?"

STAND

In situations man will take a stand
But, God always has the final plan
Never make a permanent decision
In a temporary situation
Take a stand and do the best that you can

Things will become rough and tough
But, God will work it out
Problems may have you running
Here, there, around and about
But, always choose God's route

When you feel that you are all alone
Remember! God's present is known
Crying may endure for a night
Share those tears, it's alright
In the morning, you will see the light

It is good to take a stand
As long as you are under God's command
You would never know where you may land
So put God first in all of your plans
Because you are always safe in His hands

Stand: To be in a particular condition or state.

Joshua 1:5 "There shall not any man be able to **_stand_** before thee all the days of thy life; as I was with Moses,"

BLINDSIDE

Who are those people looking at me?
My eyes are wide open, yet I cannot see
They are saying something and I agree
My heart is clear and my mind is free
My hearing is sharper, but I still can't see

Who are there, I plea
I can feel them looking at me
To see them, this will never be
My world is dark, I cannot see

Losing my sight, my hearing has double
My Godly strength, keeps me out of trouble
I take my ears and eyes everywhere I go
When asked, what life has for me, my God would know

Blinded: Deprive someone of understanding, judgment, or perception.

John 12:40   "HE HATH ***BLINDED*** THEIR EYES, AND HARDENED THEIR HEART; THAT THEY SHALL NOT SEE WITH THEIR EYES, NOR UNDERSTAND WITH THEIR HEART, AND BE CONVERTE, AND I SHALL HEAL THEM."

GOOD TEACHERS

Teachers are pairs of eyes that watches you each day
Sets of ears listening to what you have to say
You must do the right thing before and after the bell rings
In their classes, be careful of the things that you bring
Anything tasteless comes out when they speak or sing

They stand firm and willing to do
Whenever they hear the command from you
In K through two they teach them how to tie their shoes
Grades three to eight, they learn the golden rules
From nine to twelve, they think of teachers as fools

Deep in their minds, teachers are wiser than owls
If parents cut out the negative, the students will bloom like wildflowers
They hear and see everything in the class that you do
It never gets out of proportion until parents lend a hand or two
Certain things that parents say or do may hurt you

Good teachers are very hard to find
Parents those are the ones you want to stand behind
When dealing with students and parents, teachers need to unwind
Relax, while in school with their teachers, your children are fine

Teachers: Somebody who teaches, especially as a profession.

1 Chronicles 25:8   "And they cast lots, ward against ward, as well the small as the great, the **_teacher_** as the scholar."

LATERAL ENTRY TEACHER

So you went to college, total years of four
To become a teacher you need to do more
Don't look at it as a free ride
It is a profession that requires you to be certified

Regular or lateral, there is no difference in the two
Both are teachers and equal work is required of you
Lateral teachers work as hard or harder everyday
They are considered teachers and draw equal pay

It's hard to digest bad things that people may say
With a little more effort you will get through each day
Reports are due without delay
Grading those test papers, leaves not time for play

When you see your first students after they are all grown
Doctors, lawyers, bankers, writers, and so on….
Teachers with children of their own
Your job as a lateral entry teacher is well shown

English teachers taught writers how to write
Social studies teachers taught lawyers how to fight
Math teachers taught bankers how to count right
Lateral Entry Teacher taught us that everything will be alright

Miracle: Beating the odds.

John 3:2   "The same came to Jesus by night and said unto him, Rabbi, we know that thou art a teacher come from God: for no man can do these ***miracles*** that thou doest, except God be with him."

SISTERS

You are my sister and my friend
Dual relationship that God has send
Very special bond until the end
Only death can tear or mend

Sharing a lifetime of love
Not carried by a dove
But, ascended from above
Stay sweet and kind beloved

As sisters, we did our best
Loving each other was the real test
Getting there was a hard quest
Finally, we can sit back and rest

The holidays is a wonderful time
Now that we are in our prime
Relax with a glass of iced tea with lemon-lime
Thanking God for another day of sunshine

Sisters: A female who has the same parent(s).

John 11:1   "Now a certain man was sick named Laz'-a-rus, of Beth'-a-ny, the town of Mary and her *__sister__* Martha."

HOMELESS

Hey man can you spare a dime
Yes brother sharing is not a crime
Thank you for your money and time
Life was great at onetime
This was before I hit my prime

I went from a Lawyer working full-time
Dropped to a Bagger part-time
Currently, I feel worst than slime
Living my life on borrowed time
Hit rock bottom that resulted from a rapid climb

Don't ever think that you are exempt
Because life will throw you a wrench
That will leave you in a deep trench
Clueless and empty without a clench
Careful, it can be you sitting on that bench

Beggar: Somebody who begs fro money or food from strangers.

Luke 16:20   "And there was a certain ___beggar___ named Laz'-a-rus, which was laid at his gate, full of sores."

STARTING OVER

If you think that starting life all over is going to be fun
Just the thought of it, makes you want to run
The smallest details are hotter than the sun
It makes you wonder, how it all begun

Memories of your earlier age, you would have to be spoon-fed
Coming from someone else, you can be falsely led
Writing the truth is like bumping your head
Questioning each word every time it is read

From birth to two, someone did everything for you
From combing your hair to tying your shoes
At three you were not even in life's core
Still not there, at the age of four

Five you can remember some of the pain
Six you have something to gain
Seven to twelve memories resides in your brain
Thirteen to eighteen, life for you is no longer plain

Now you are looking for answers and beginning to complain
Your future depends on the truth and someone needs to explain
To know who you are, you have to cling
To something from the past, even the smallest thing

To you anything familiar would have a ring
You will be surprise what the next level brings
Sometimes we all have to cry even queens and kings
Past and present broken hearts, wait to see what the future brings

Memory: The knowledge or impression that somebody retains of a particular person, event, period, or subject.

Proverbs 10:7   "The _**memory**_ of the just is blessed: but the name of the wicked shall rot."

OLD AGE

Aging is inevitable, yet a scary role
Here is a story that should always be told:
As the saying goes, we will never be whole
Until we learn the beauty of getting old

It is a time that our entire life begins to unfold
Our body temperature goes from hot to cold
Over fifty and we think of our ages as gold
Yet, we are afraid of getting old

Years after years, we think of aging as a race
We all started out with life on first base
Lived it day by day through God's Grace
Running until we reach our resting place

Aging is like a merry-go-round, so discreet
A place where your younger and older ages meet
Things from your early life, you will eventually reap
Your entire childhood life will be a repeat

It is like a telephone, yet you cannot re-dial
Getting old means once a man and twice a child
When you accept the beauty of getting old
You would age gracefully and become whole

Old Age: Consists of ages nearing or surpassing the life expectancy of human beings.

Genesis 17:11 "Now Abraham and Sarah were **_old_** and well stricken in **_age_**; and it ceased to be with Sarah after the manner of women."

MIRROR IMAGES

When I experience life's woes, I say; why me
Past events that took place, I can now clearly see
Memories are images that linger for years unbound
My own face is distorted, yet my mind is sound
But in that mirror, the true me, can be found

Before, I could not see myself in others situation
But, time presented me with an unannounced invitation
Several things in my past, I can give a semi-account
Because in my repertoire, the past still counts
Various things rather they made me happy, sad, or even shout

Looking in the mirror at myself so hard to bare
It is so painful; that I refuse to take the dare
Even the thought creates a tremendous scare
Regaining my normal life back is rare
So, I will force myself and take the dare

Looking in the present mirror the only person that I see is me
This person helps me figure things out to make me free
The real person in the mirror is very honest as far as I can see
Connecting my inner spirit with that person is the key
My soul is beginning to open up and my life has taken on a new decree

Experience: The knowledge of and skill in something gained throug**h being involved** involved in it or exposed to it over a period of time."

Genesis 30:27   "I have learned by ***experience*** that the LORD hath blessed me for thy sake."

WHEN A STRANGER CALLS

When a stranger calls, don't hang up
Listen and see what that call is all about
You would be surprise what you find out
That person dialed your number without a doubt
Life for you was about to change its route

Maybe that call was not for you
After listening, it gave you something to do
The initial call you did not know one another
Attempted to hang-up, but said why bother
The voice started off soft, but got louder

It gave you instructions step by step
Described your life to the deepest depth
This stranger's advice; you had to accept
Conveyed memories in your heart that you kept
From that point on, it affected how you slept

Certain conversations can affect you a lot
Especially old devils that you have fought
Painful buried things that by now should have rot
Reopening old wounds may leave you distraught
Before you answer that phone, give it a second thought

Stranger: A person whom one does not know or with whom one is not familiar.

Ruth 2:10   "Why have I found grace in thine eyes, that thou shouldest take knowledge of me, seeing I am a ***stranger***?"

LEADERSHIP

A good leader leads himself first
Then others follow his lead
A position does not make the leader
The leader makes the position
He allows nothing to control him
He is not better than his workers
He would not ask them to do something
That he would not do himself

A good leader keeps you from going astray
Firm with the workers and do not play
Manages the firm professional day after day
Guides and supports the workers all the way
Direct, prompt, and consistent and without delay
Headship his personal life everyday
With strict tact ness, whereas everyone can say
Personal and professional leadership is here to stay

Leader: Person who leads or commands a group, organization, or country.

Isaiah 55:4   "Behold, I have given him for a witness to the people, a ***leader*** and commander to the people."

MENTAL CLOSET

You should periodically clean your mental closet
Before you go ballistic, and don't even know what caused it

Organize, polish, dispose, and donate
Just eliminate the junk before it is to late

Half of the junk does not belong to you anyway
So why hold on to them year after year, day after day

More than half of the junk it belongs to someone other than you
That was collected during the past five years or two

For years, you took other people situations
And turn them into problems of damnation

By the use of your itchy ears and uncontrollable mouth
You built on problems that will eventually make you shout

You store these poisons in your head
Overly stress, burnt out, and soon to be dead

You must clean your mental close at the end of each day
Properly place them where they belongs, out of your way

Recycle them back to their owners and let them stay
Do not take on ownership because you will become their prey

Breath a breathe of fresh air into your mental closet every minute
At the end of the day your heart will have joy, love, and peace in it

Mind: The center of consciousness that generates thoughts, feelings, ideas, and perceptions and stores knowledge and memories.

Job 23:13   "But he is in one ***mind*** and who can turn him?"

ENDURANCE

In this world, we did not ask for certain things
It is beyond us what life tends to bring
Life teaches us everything that we need to know
To get this knowledge we don't have to go door to door
Then keep living because life's experience teaches us more

It has been said that some people are born blessed
Some with a silver spoon in their mouths
Fitted to sit on a throne like kings and queens
Others with a veil over the face
Still life is granted to everyone by pure grace

Life is unique because it has its own golden rule
We cannot learn it even if we spend our entire lives in school
Others, that are environmentally gifted, known as street smart
Both groups began at the point that marked START
Endurance is a life-long lesson for living that plays a special part

Endure: To experience exertion, pain, or hardship without giving up.

Matthew 24:13   "But he that shall ***endure*** unto the end, the same shall be saved."

FAMILY

Family is a word that is hard to define
A total stranger is usually more kind
Kinfolks is what it suppose to be
But they don't act like it, at least not to me
Relatives are suppose to laugh and have fun
Children can express themselves, play, and run
When it comes to adults, family unity, we have none

If our ancestors were able to talk
They would turn away and take a walk
Family knows who they are kin too
All of your life, they knew of or about you
Our forefathers, we can never walk in their shoes
When it comes to family, we don't have a clue
Real family, there are still a few

Family should always have our backs
Especially when we are under attack
Yet, togetherness is something that they lack
They have no compassion, and that's a fact
Division is all that they know and that's that
We refuse to take care of one another
Constant fights between sisters and brothers

Creating hatred instead of fun
Attacking each other with loaded guns
Close knit family is a thing of the past
But, our relatives and kinfolks will forever last
But, there are no expressions of love you see
Never on one accord and very rarely agree
Do to the lack of unconditional love and Family unity

Unity: The state of being one.

Psalms 133:1   "Behold, how good and how pleasant it is for brethren to dwell together in ***unity***."

MAKING DECISIONS

When it comes to making life long decisions
Be careful who you ask because it may cause some division
Most problems can be resolved without rescission
Should you turn to your friends or to your religion?
The solution is to look to God before making any decision

It is hard to identify life's pressures
Especially when we look to others for gestures
Regrouping can be a great refresher
Good as well as bad deed can be a thresher
But a fervent prayer would be more fresher

Consequences can cause a great deal of trouble
To the point whereas your problems may double
Simple life can sometimes become saddle
So mixed-up, out-of-control is a case of pure rubble
Rethink, start-over, this time, be more humble

It is all right to make a decision on any given day
Pray, if the timing is not right, you need to walk away
Decisions are not based on the things that you say
Don't look at life as black or white, but gray
The spiritual side of life is usually the right way

Decision: The process of coming to a conclusion or determination about
something.

Job 3:14   "Multitudes, multitudes in the valley of decisions: for the day
of the LORD is near in the valley of ***decision***."

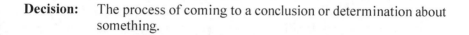

DREAMS

Dreams are the reverberation during sleep
Sounds that is vibrant, yet so sweet
An echo that travels from our heads to our feet
Unknown faces that we would never meet
It takes us places we never vision that we would go
They bring messages, open doorways, and so much more
Takes us on journeys that we may or may not have been before

Everything that we dream about are suppose to be a part of us
It has been scientifically proven, so why make a fuss
We can visualize, revisit, analyze, and discuss
But our dreams are based on belief and trust
The vital messages tells us something about our life
Good or bad we must receive what it has bring without a fight
If not, it will reappear in the same form night after night

Dream warnings come with anxiety or outright fear
Running from it or being scared, don't try it dear
They will reoccur night after night and rather clear
With a more visible and sturdy stare
Dreams are early cures for things that have happen or probably would
Useful techniques such as guided imagery and therapy should
True revelation of our dreams should be clear and well understood

Dreams: Successions of images, ideas, emotions, and sensations that occur involuntary in the mind during certain stages of sleep.

Daniel 1:17 "God gave them knowledge and skill in all learning and wisdom: and Daniel had understanding in all visions and ___dreams___."

YES

Remember! For every one YES there are a hundred NO
It takes a lot of NO's to get you where you want to go
Unlike a NO, a YES takes its time and it comes real slow
When waiting for a positive answer, you need to know
That a negative answer can take you for a real blow

That job that you want the first answer is usually a NO
Don't quit because opportunity is still knocking at your door
When that special job comes, you would know it for sure
That one yes made up for that hundred no's
Patience is a virtue, that's one thing that we defiantly know

Whatever you do, you should always do your best
Time and endurance is truly the real test
Pray a strong prayer and send up a fervent request
Be honest and sincere and God will do the rest
The final decision is God's eventually He will say yes

Opportunity: A chance, especially one that offers some kind of advantage.

Galatians 6:10   "As we have therefore ***opportunity***, let us do good unto all men,"

GOD

God is always with us through thick and thin
Regardless how many times that we have sinned
He is our sunshine and our rain
Even when we are well or going through pain

God always hears our thoughts and cries
Both in our comings and our goodbyes
His prophecy will be fulfill both in you and I
Either while we are living or after we die

God is firm and stands on his word
He cares for us as well as the birds
He is keeper of all, haven't you heard
Read your Bible, He says it all in red words

Word or Word of God: Christianity, the Bible or Scripture, considered as revealing divine truth.

John 1:1   "In the beginning was the *Word,* and the Word was with God, and the *Word was God*."

GOD REIGNS

God is God all by himself at every level
He needs no help from us not even the Devil
Awesome, He reigns from the Heavens above
He showers us with His power, wisdom, and love

Oh how visible is God's sovereignty
Blind to man's perplexed scrutiny
He reigns on the just and unjust
What does it takes for you to gain His trust

God gave us the wonderful rain
Which once destroyed the world
He sealed it with a promised to Noah
That He would never do it again

God reigns on everything that we endures
He is always present and that's for sure
Believe in Him forever and forever more
For He is Alpha and Omega and He; I adore

Omega: Omega (Ω or ω)), are the last letter of the Greek alphabet, and an appellation of Christ or of God in the Book of Revelation.

Revelation 1:8   "I am ***Alpha and Omega***, the beginning and the ending, saith the Lord, which is to come, the Almighty."

THE OLD TESTAMENT

(Alpha)

GENESIS The first Book of the Bible written by Moses. The name (Gen•e•sis) Is derived from the Greek word meaning "origin" or "beginning." Which is the story of the creation of the world was told. Consists of 50 chapters: 1:1 – 50:26

1:1 "In the beginning God created the heavens and the earth."

50:26 "So Joseph died, being an hundred and ten years old: and embalmed him, and he was put in a coffin in Egypt".

THE NEW TESTAMENT

(Omega)

Revelation   The sixty-sixth Book of the Bible, written by John. It promises (Rev•e•la•tion) that God will institute universal peace, prosperity and cooperation over all the earth immediately after the return of Jesus Christ. It reveals how this wonderful new world will be established and why it will never be destroyed or super- seded by any other way of life or social order. Consists of 22 chapters: 1:1 – 22:21

1:1   "THE Revelation of Jesus Christ, which God gave unto him, to shew unto his servants things which must shortly come to pass;

and he sent and signified it by his angel unto his servant John:"

22:21   "The grace of our Lord, Jesus Christ *be* with you all. A-men'."

GLOSSARY

Alpha - First or most important

Adhere – Hold firmly to a belief, idea, or opinion

Anointed – Smear or rub with oil, typically in a religious ceremony

Bondage -- Condition of being controlled by something that limits freedom

Covenant – Solemn agreement that is binding on all parties

Crucify – Execute somebody by crucifixion

Decree -- The will or purpose of God

Destined – Sure, preordained, or intended

Divine -- Being God or a god or goddess

Domain – The scope of a subject

Eternal – God as a universal spirit

Inherit – Become the owner of something when somebody dies

Ordinance - Holy Communion ceremony

Perish – Come to an end or cease to exist

Radiant – Express joy, energy, or good health in a pleasing way

Omega – The end, or the last

GOD – One supreme being in the form of three persons, Father, Son, and Holy Ghost

All definitions were taken from the World English Dictionary and Wikipedia

Printed in the United States
By Bookmasters